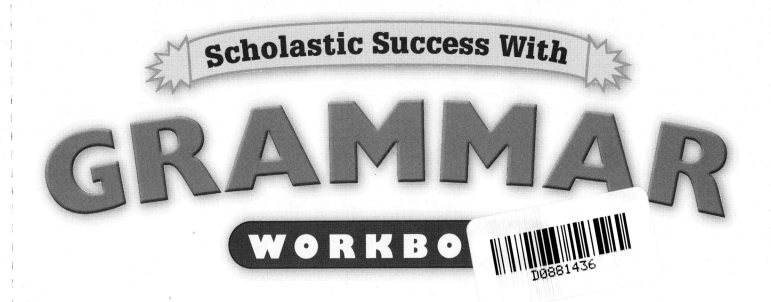

Scholastic Success With GRAMMAR WORKBOOK

GRADE 5

SCHOLASTIC PROFESSIONAL BOOKS

New York • Toronto • London • Auckland • Sydney • Mexico City
New Delhi • Hong Kong • Buenos Aires

Cover design by Maria Lilja
Cover artwork by Victoria Raymond

ISBN: 0-439-43402-5
Copyright © 2002 by Scholastic Inc.
All rights reserved. Published by Scholastic Inc.
Printed in the U.S.A.

3 4 5 6 7 8 9 10   40   09 08 07 06 05 05 03

TABLE OF CONTENTS

INTRODUCTION

"Nothing Succeeds Like Success."
—Alexandre Dumas the Elder, 1854

And no other resource boosts kids' grammar skills like *Scholastic Success With Grammar*! For classroom or at-home use, this exciting series for kids in grades 1 through 6 provides invaluable reinforcement and practice in grammar topics such as:

- sentence types
- parts of speech
- common and proper nouns
- sentence structure
- verb tenses
- subject-verb agreement
- punctuation
- capitalization
- and more!

Each 64-page book contains loads of clever practice pages to keep kids challenged and excited as they strengthen the grammar skills they need to read and write well.

For almost every topic, you'll also find an assessment page that gives kids realistic practice in taking standardized tests—and helps you see their progress!

What makes *Scholastic Success With Grammar* so solid?
Each practice page in the series reinforces a specific, age-appropriate skill as outlined in one or more of the following standardized tests:

- Iowa Tests of Basic Skills
- California Tests of Basic Skills
- California Achievement Test
- Metropolitan Achievement Test
- Stanford Achievement Test

Take the lead and help kids succeed with *Scholastic Success With Grammar*. Parents and teachers agree: No one helps kids succeed like Scholastic.

TYPES OF SENTENCES

RETEACHING: A **declarative** sentence makes a statement and ends with a period. An **interrogative** sentence asks a question and ends with a question mark. An **imperative** sentence gives a command and ends with a period or an exclamation point. An **exclamatory** sentence shows strong feeling and ends with an exclamation mark.

A. Identify each type of sentence by writing *declarative, interrogative, imperative,* or *exclamatory* on the line.

1. Are you ready to write a story? _____

2. I need help! _____

3. Not every story gets printed. _____

4. Tell me a good ending. _____

5. We ate salad and roast beef. _____

6. I couldn't wait for lunch! _____

B. Read each group of words below. If it has a subject and a predicate and expresses a complete thought, write *complete* on the line. If it is not a complete sentence, write *incomplete.*

1. With my fork. _____

2. She liked my poem. _____

3. Was proud. _____

4. I'll write another letter. _____

C. Rewrite the incomplete thoughts from Part B to make complete sentences. Remember to capitalize and punctuate correctly.

_____

_____

_____

_____

TYPES OF SENTENCES

A. Rewrite each sentence, using capitalization and the correct end punctuation. Then write *declarative, interrogative, imperative,* **or** *exclamatory* **to tell what kind of sentence each one is.**

> **RETEACHING:** A **declarative** sentence makes a statement and ends with a period. An **interrogative** sentence asks a question and ends with a question mark. An **imperative** sentence gives a command and ends with a period or an exclamation point. An **exclamatory** sentence shows strong feeling and ends with an exclamation mark.

1. do you like to write poems

_____   _____

2. I can't believe my story won

_____   _____

3. he asked me a lot of questions

_____   _____

4. write back to me soon

_____   _____

B. Write about an animal that interests you. Use each phrase in the type of sentence shown in parentheses ( ).

1. (Declarative) I know about _____

2. (Exclamatory) That's the best _____

3. (Interrogative) Where is _____

4. (Imperative) Tell me _____

TYPES OF SENTENCES

Read each sentence. Decide how the underlined words should be written. Fill in the bubble next to your answer.

1. Go to the library and check out a few books on <u>wolves?</u>

   ⓐ wolves!

   ⓑ wolves.

   ⓒ correct as is

2. <u>you will learn</u> that the gray wolf and the red wolf are distant relatives of domestic dogs.

   ⓐ You will learn

   ⓑ Will you learn

   ⓒ correct as is

3. <u>a wolf will</u> not attack a human unless it is provoked.

   ⓐ Will a wolf

   ⓑ A wolf will

   ⓒ correct as is

4. Tell me what wolves eat besides <u>rabbits.</u>

   ⓐ rabbits?

   ⓑ rabbits!

   ⓒ correct as is

5. <u>wolves</u> eat deer, snakes, insects, and sometimes fruit?

   ⓐ Do wolves

   ⓑ Wolves

   ⓒ correct as is

6. What an eerie sound a wolf howl <u>is!</u>

   ⓐ is?

   ⓑ is

   ⓒ correct as is

7. <u>red wolves are</u> being bred in zoos because the wolf is almost extinct.

   ⓐ Are red wolves

   ⓑ Red wolves are

   ⓒ correct as is

8. What happens to the red wolves when they're old enough to care for <u>themselves.</u>

   ⓐ themselves?

   ⓑ themselves!

   ⓒ correct as is

9. The young wolves are released in <u>forests.</u>

   ⓐ forests?

   ⓑ forests!

   ⓒ correct as is

10. Working with wolves is such an <u>interesting job</u>

    ⓐ interesting job!

    ⓑ interesting job?

    ⓒ correct as is

COMPLETE AND SIMPLE SUBJECTS

RETEACHING: The **complete subject** is all the words in the subject of a sentence. The **simple subject** is the main word or words in the subject of the sentence. It tells who or what the sentence is about.

A. Draw a line between the subject and the predicate of each sentence.

1. This story tells about Jamie and Grama Bowman.

2. Grama Bowman used to tell Jamie stories.

3. Jamie's great-grandmother loved to see the fox's tracks.

4. Her best friend, Wokwses the Fox, left the tracks.

5. That clever fox delighted Grama.

6. Grama's song is a kind of fox song.

B. Underline the complete subject once and the simple subject twice.

1. The autumn leaves were blowing in the wind.

2. The old Indian people told a story about the leaves.

3. The fall season is the time for leaf dances.

4. The leaves put on their best colors at that time.

5. The cold, autumn wind comes to take them.

6. Grama Bowman, a wise woman, told Jamie this.

7. The old leaves are like old people.

8. Their final dances are very beautiful.

9. The very best dances occur in autumn.

10. Grama Bowman's story explains a natural event.

COMPLETE AND SIMPLE SUBJECTS

A. Read the sentences below. Underline each complete subject once.

1. Old, wise Grama Bowman teaches Jamie a song.

2. The first line of the song is "Hey, kwah nu deh."

3. The words of the song repeat.

4. This song, a kind of chant, stays in Jamie's memory forever.

5. Her dream includes this song.

6. A fox with glistening eyes appears in the answer to the song.

7. The fox, a mysterious animal, disappears again.

B. Read the sentences below. Underline each simple subject twice.

1. The events in Jamie's dream tell a great deal.

2. Her conversations in the dream show her relationship to Grama Bowman.

3. Their actions reveal a loving closeness.

4. Jamie, Grama Bowman's great granddaughter, learns from her.

5. Both characters enjoy each other's company.

6. Grama's lessons to her will live on in Jamie's memory.

7. Grama Bowman, a guide and teacher, shares her knowledge.

8. The world of nature is Grama's home.

COMPLETE AND SIMPLE SUBJECTS

A. Fill in the bubble next to the complete subject of each sentence.

1. Jamie's great-grandmother was an Abenaki Indian.
   - ⓐ Jamie's great-grandmother
   - ⓑ Abenaki Indian
   - ⓒ great-grandmother

2. This old woman moved in with Jamie's family.
   - ⓐ woman
   - ⓑ old woman
   - ⓒ This old woman

3. Their house on the Winooski River had a maple woods behind it.
   - ⓐ Winooski River
   - ⓑ Their house on the Winooski River
   - ⓒ had a maple woods

4. The woods up the hill contained birch trees.
   - ⓐ The woods
   - ⓑ contained birch trees
   - ⓒ The woods up the hill

5. Sweet, wild blueberries grew there.
   - ⓐ blueberries
   - ⓑ Sweet, wild blueberries
   - ⓒ wild blueberries

B. Fill in the bubble next to the simple subject of each sentence.

1. Early settlers from France learned from the Abenaki Indians.
   - ⓐ settlers
   - ⓑ France
   - ⓒ Early settlers from France

2. The Native Americans taught the settlers about blueberries.
   - ⓐ Americans
   - ⓑ The Native Americans
   - ⓒ Native Americans

3. The dead blueberry bushes are burned each fall.
   - ⓐ blueberry
   - ⓑ are burned
   - ⓒ bushes

4. The new, green plants will be stronger in the spring.
   - ⓐ green plants
   - ⓑ plants
   - ⓒ spring

5. Proper care of plants makes a difference.
   - ⓐ care
   - ⓑ makes
   - ⓒ plants

COMPLETE AND SIMPLE PREDICATES

A. Underline the complete predicate once and the simple predicate twice. Then write *A* if the simple predicate is an action verb, or *B* if it is a state-of-being verb.

1. Listening to the radio is popular among my classmates. _____

2. My friends and I listen to the latest pop music on the radio. _____

3. Our class danced in the gym last Friday afternoon. _____

4. Some of the teachers at the dance sang some "oldies." _____

5. The dance was a huge success among students and teachers. _____

6. Some parents stood along the side of the gym. _____

7. They seemed amused by the music and dancing. _____

B. For each complete subject, write a complete predicate. Then underline the complete predicate once and the simple predicate twice. Use action verbs and state-of-being verbs.

1. My fifth-grade class _____

_____

2. Some of the younger students in my school _____

_____

3. My favorite book _____

_____

4. The movie _____

_____

COMPLETE AND SIMPLE PREDICATES

> **RETEACHING:** The **complete predicate** is all the words in the predicate of a sentence. It tells what the subject does or is. The **simple predicate** is the main word in the complete predicate. It shows an action or state of being.

A. Read the sentences below. Underline each complete predicate once.

1. The game against the Kansas City Royals would start soon.

2. The left fielder was running out to the field beside Ken.

3. A tingle of excitement ran down Ken junior's back.

4. The new left fielder was none other than his dad.

5. The crowd at the stadium let out a roar.

6. All the fans, in the stadium and out of it, knew this was a great moment.

7. Ken, the left fielder's son, felt so happy!

B. Read the sentences below. Underline each simple predicate twice.

1. I read the story of Ken Griffey, Junior and Senior.

2. These two famous players are father and son.

3. They even played on the same team together.

4. Both men were in the Seattle Mariners line-up.

5. This father-son team made history.

6. The President of the United States sent them a telegram after one great game.

7. The Griffeys appeared together on a few television shows.

8. These two great athletes remain famous today.

On a separate piece of paper, write about something you enjoy doing with your family. Underline each complete predicate once and each simple predicate twice.

COMPLETE AND SIMPLE PREDICATES

A. Read each sentence. Fill in the bubble next to the complete predicate.

1. Our fifth-grade class performed a musical Friday.

   (a) fifth-grade class

   (b) performed a musical Friday

   (c) performed

2. Parents and teachers attended the event, too.

   (a) attended the event, too

   (b) attended

   (c) Parents and teachers

3. Mr. Stein, our teacher, was the musical director.

   (a) Mr. Stein, our teacher

   (b) was the musical director

   (c) the musical director

4. He also chose the musical numbers.

   (a) He also chose

   (b) chose

   (c) chose the musical numbers

5. Some of us worked behind the scenes.

   (a) worked behind the scenes

   (b) Some of us

   (c) worked

B. Read each sentence. Fill in the bubble next to the simple predicate.

1. Some students were in charge of building the stage sets.

   (a) Some students

   (b) were

   (c) in charge of

2. Others collected costumes.

   (a) collected

   (b) collected costumes

   (c) Others

3. Any kind of performance is definitely a group effort!

   (a) performance

   (b) is definitely

   (c) is

4. Everyone was a little nervous before the performance.

   (a) was

   (b) Everyone

   (c) nervous

5. Mr. Stein congratulated us after the thunderous applause.

   (a) thunderous applause

   (b) Mr. Stein

   (c) congratulated

COMPOUND SUBJECTS AND PREDICATES

A. If the sentence has a compound subject, underline each simple subject once. Circle the conjunction. If the sentence has a compound predicate, underline each verb twice. Circle the conjunction.

1. Families and friends often help each other during times of hardship.

2. During a war, people sometimes leave their homes and lose their belongings.

3. Intelligence, courage, and luck can help people survive.

4. Food and clean water may become scarce.

5. Many young people join the army or work in factories.

B. Read each pair of sentences. Then combine them to form a compound subject or a compound predicate. Write your new sentence on the line.

1. Annemarie played with the dolls. Ellen played with the dolls.

   _____

2. Kirsti cried about the shoes. Kirsti complained about the shoes.

   _____

3. Annemarie brushed her hair. Annemarie handed the brush to Ellen.

   _____

4. Families hid in the house. Families fled to the forest.

   _____

COMPOUND SUBJECTS AND PREDICATES

A. Read the sentences. Underline compound subjects once and compound predicates twice. Circle the conjunctions.

1. Annemarie and Ellen are good friends.

2. Their homes and families are in Denmark.

3. The girls sometimes talk or giggle with Annemarie's sister.

4. All three children joke, laugh, and play games together.

5. The Rosens or the Johansens will be there.

6. Families and friends help each other in time of war.

7. The Johansens hide Ellen and keep her safe.

8. Ellen reads and sings to Kirsti.

9. Denmark, Holland, and other countries struggled during the war.

10. People succeed or fail in surprising ways.

B. Select two sentences from Part A, one with a compound subject and one with a compound predicate. Rewrite each sentence with your own compound subject or predicate.

_____

_____

_____

_____

On a separate piece of paper, write a paragraph about someone who might help you carry out a difficult task. Tell what they might do. Use compound subjects and predicates.

Name _____

COMPOUND SUBJECTS AND PREDICATES

A. Decide if the underlined part of each sentence is correct.
Fill in the bubble next to the correct answer.

1. I, George, and Tina are playground monitors.
   - ⓐ George and I and Tina
   - ⓑ George, Tina, and I
   - ⓒ correct as is

2. We watch for problems and solve them.
   - ⓐ watch solve for problems,
   - ⓑ watch for problems or solve.
   - ⓒ correct as is

3. Keith and Tracy asked me for help with a problem.
   - ⓐ Keith, and Tracy
   - ⓑ Keith, Tracy
   - ⓒ correct as is

4. Their friend Matt hit a ball lost it on the school roof.
   - ⓐ hit a ball, lost it
   - ⓑ hit a ball and lost it
   - ⓒ correct as is

5. I and Tina found Matt in a corner of the playground.
   - ⓐ Tina and I
   - ⓑ I or Tina
   - ⓒ correct as is

6. He pointed showed us where it went.
   - ⓐ pointed and showed us
   - ⓑ pointed or showed us
   - ⓒ correct as is

7. Tina looked up, turned, walked over to Ms. Weiss.
   - ⓐ looked up, turned, and walked
   - ⓑ looked up and turned, walked
   - ⓒ correct as is

8. Ms. Weiss joined us or helped with the discussion.
   - ⓐ joined us and helped
   - ⓑ joined us, helped
   - ⓒ correct as is

9. Ms. Weiss said we could get the custodian, find another ball.
   - ⓐ get the custodian, and find
   - ⓑ get the custodian or find
   - ⓒ correct as is

10. Matt smiled and went to find the custodian.
    - ⓐ smiled, and went to find
    - ⓑ smiled and, went to find
    - ⓒ correct as is

COMPOUND SENTENCES

A. Circle the conjunction in parentheses ( ) that makes sense. Then rewrite the sentence using the conjunction.

1. I want to go to the movies, _____ my friend Pat does not. (or, but)

   _____

2. It rained last night, _____ we had to stay home. (and, but)

   _____

3. Ed will drive to Texas, _____ he will take the train. (or, and)

   _____

4. It snowed this morning, _____ the sun came out this afternoon. (but, or)

   _____

B. Write a compound sentence from the two simple sentences. Use the conjunction shown in parentheses ( ).

1. We wanted to ride our bikes home. Mine had a flat tire. (but)

   _____

2. The whistle blew. The train pulled out of the station. (and)

   _____

3. I will finish the job today. Bob will finish it tomorrow. (or)

   _____

COMPOUND SENTENCES

RETEACHING: A compound **sentence** is a sentence made up of two independent thoughts joined by a comma and the conjunction *and*, *but*, or *or*.

A. In the space provided, combine each pair of sentences into one compound sentence. Use a comma and choose the conjunction (*and*, *but*, or *or*) that makes the most sense.

1. Our cousins arrived. We were very happy to see them.

   _____

2. Eileen had cut her hair short. Her twin sister Emily still had long hair.

   _____

3. They had always looked exactly alike. I could not get used to them!

   _____

4. Would they play with me? Would they play only with my older sisters?

   _____

5. First Eileen gave me a hug. Then Emily did the same.

   _____

6. Our parents went into the kitchen to talk. The rest of us preferred to be outside.

   _____

7. We used to have a hiding place. I was not sure if Eileen and Emily would remember it.

   _____

8. At dinner, Mom said the twins could stay with us. We could go stay with them.

   _____

   _____

B. Write a paragraph about a skill or sport you have learned. Use different types of sentences to make your writing interesting.

   _____

   _____

   _____

   _____

COMPOUND SENTENCES

Decide if there is an error in the underlined part of each compound sentence. Fill in the bubble next to the correct answer.

1. We cleaned our house last <u>weekend and I</u> threw out some old books and toys.

   (a) weekend but I
   (b) weekend, and I
   (c) correct as is

2. Old toys went in a big plastic <u>bag, but old books</u> went in a box.

   (a) bag, old books
   (b) bag or old books
   (c) correct as is

3. I could have cleared my book <u>shelf, and I</u> wanted to keep a few old favorites.

   (a) shelf, but I
   (b) shelf, And I
   (c) correct as is

4. I gave some toys to a <u>neighbor but, most</u> went to the thrift store.

   (a) neighbor, but most
   (b) neighbor and most
   (c) correct as is

5. We drove to the thrift <u>store, and I</u> helped carry the boxes inside.

   (a) store and I
   (b) store, But I
   (c) correct as is

6. I wanted to look around the <u>store but we</u> didn't have time.

   (a) store and we
   (b) store, but we
   (c) correct as is

7. I saw an old typewriter <u>there, and no one</u> uses those things anymore!

   (a) there, but no one
   (b) there but No one
   (c) correct as is

8. We stopped at the <u>library, and each of</u> us checked out some books.

   (a) library, Each
   (b) library and each
   (c) correct as is

9. My shelves looked <u>empty, the library books</u> helped fill them up a little.

   (a) empty, but the library books
   (b) empty, or the library books
   (c) correct as is

10. I loved my old <u>books but, my interests</u> have changed as I've gotten older.

    (a) books but my interests
    (b) books, but my interests
    (c) correct as is

COMMON AND PROPER NOUNS

A. Read the sentences below. Underline any common nouns in each sentence once and any proper nouns twice.

1. Mr. Sherlock Holmes is a famous fictional detective.

2. This character was created by the author Sir Arthur Conan Doyle.

3. Holmes appeared in 56 stories and several novels written by Doyle, including *The Sign of Four*.

4. He was often assisted by his friend Dr. John Watson.

5. They worked together on mysteries throughout the city of London.

B. Read the sentences below. Identify the underlined words in each sentence as proper or common nouns.

1. <u>Peter Jones</u> is a <u>detective</u> who works at <u>Scotland Yard</u>.

   _____

2. Yesterday <u>Mr. Reginald Merryweather</u> came to him with a very strange <u>story</u>.

   _____

3. It seems that rare <u>coins</u> are missing from the <u>Bank of London</u> where he works.

   _____

4. The <u>money</u> was kept in a <u>safe</u> at the <u>bank</u>.

   _____

5. <u>Peter Jones</u> decided to call <u>Sherlock Holmes</u> to assist him with the <u>case</u>.

   _____

COMMON AND PROPER NOUNS

A. Read the following sentences. Circle the proper noun(s) in each sentence and then write what it names on the line. The first one has been done for you.

1. I read the *Dallas Morning News* every day. _____*newspaper*_____

2. We have two dogs, named Archie and Samantha. _____

3. In the fall, I will attend Nichols Middle School. _____

4. We are going to read about the Industrial Revolution. _____

5. Did you have a good time at our Fourth of July picnic this year? _____

6. I want to join the National Geographic Society. _____

B. Complete the chart by filling in each missing common or proper noun. The first one has been done for you.

Common Noun	Proper Noun
newspaper	*Daily News*
era	
	Chicago
pet	
president	
	Memorial Day
	Best Toy, Inc.

COMMON AND PROPER NOUNS

Decide if there is an error in the underlined nouns. Fill in the bubble next to the correct answer.

1. I think <u>aunt Anita</u> made tacos.

   ⓐ Aunt Anita

   ⓑ aunt anita

   ⓒ correct as is

2. We take a vacation in <u>Redwood National Park</u> every summer.

   ⓐ Redwood National park

   ⓑ Redwood national park

   ⓒ correct as is

3. I have a doctor's appointment on <u>tuesday, May 9</u>.

   ⓐ tuesday, may 9

   ⓑ Tuesday, May 9

   ⓒ correct as is

4. The <u>civil war</u> period is fascinating.

   ⓐ Civil war

   ⓑ Civil War

   ⓒ correct as is

5. Albert bought take-out food last night from <u>Grandma's good eats</u>.

   ⓐ Grandma's Good Eats

   ⓑ grandma's Good Eats

   ⓒ correct as is

6. Josie learned <u>French in France</u>.

   ⓐ french in France

   ⓑ french in france

   ⓒ correct as is

7. Large cats can be found in both <u>north and south America</u>.

   ⓐ North and South America

   ⓑ north and south america

   ⓒ correct as is

8. Carla moved to <u>el Paso, Texas</u>.

   ⓐ El paso, Texas

   ⓑ El Paso, Texas

   ⓒ correct as is

9. I'm planning to take a raft trip down the <u>Colorado river</u> next month.

   ⓐ Colorado River

   ⓑ colorado river

   ⓒ correct as is

10. I read an interesting story in the <u>*Houston Chronicle*</u> the other day.

    ⓐ *Houston chronicle*

    ⓑ *houston Chronicle*

    ⓒ correct as is

SINGULAR AND PLURAL NOUNS

> **RETEACHING:** A **singular noun** names one person, place, thing, or idea. A **plural noun** names more than one person, place, thing, or idea. A plural noun is most often formed by adding -s to the singular. Some nouns add -es to form the plural.

A. Read the sentences below. Circle any singular nouns in each sentence and underline any plural common nouns.

1. He loved walking in the park, taking pictures.

2. He had taken several photographs with his camera when he stopped to rest on a bench.

3. A rabbit scurried through the bushes, and several birds sang in the branches above his head.

4. Then, suddenly, two strangers came down the path and headed toward him.

5. As they ran past, they dropped some notes near his right foot.

6. He picked them up and saw that the paper was in code.

7. "I guess this is another case for the members of our agency," he said.

B. Rewrite each sentence using the plural form of the underlined nouns.

1. Ricardo snapped on the <u>light</u> and studied the coded <u>message</u>.

_____

2. Vikki gave him the <u>snapshot</u> of the <u>suspect</u>.

_____

3. He was carrying his <u>newspaper</u> and his <u>suitcase</u>.

_____

SINGULAR AND PLURAL NOUNS

RETEACHING: A **singular noun** names one person, place, or thing. A noun that names more than one is plural. A **plural noun** is often formed by adding -s or -es.

A. Underline the singular noun in each sentence.

1. My brothers and parents decided to take a scenic ride.

2. They chose a winding route that went over the mountains.

3. Of all the things they saw, a deserted mining town was the best.

4. They also saw two foxes standing near the pine tree.

5. Later, the moon made the hills and valleys glow.

6. After it was all over, the boys said, "That was a fantastic trip! Let's go again soon."

B. Underline the plural noun in each sentence.

1. Two sixth grade classes are touring our city.

2. It's amazing how interesting some of the buildings are.

3. Last week, we visited two old libraries.

4. We also saw a temple, a mosque, and two churches.

5. We also discovered a fancy iron fence and beautiful iron benches.

6. Are other cities as amazing as our city?

 On a separate piece of paper, write a brief description of some sights in your hometown. Make sure to include singular and plural nouns to describe people, places, and things.

SINGULAR AND PLURAL NOUNS

Decide if there is an error in the underlined nouns. Fill in the bubble next to the correct answer.

1. Deirdre took a trip to several <u>city</u> on the east coast last summer.

   ⓐ cities

   ⓑ citys

   ⓒ correct as is

2. Rudy saves spare change like <u>pennies</u>.

   ⓐ penny

   ⓑ pennys

   ⓒ correct as is

3. Annie bought two biscuit <u>mixs</u> when she went to the store.

   ⓐ mixes

   ⓑ mix

   ⓒ correct as is

4. We looked for different kinds of <u>shelles</u> as we walked along the beach.

   ⓐ shell

   ⓑ shells

   ⓒ correct as is

5. Quite a few <u>classes</u> in our school went on a field trip yesterday.

   ⓐ class

   ⓑ classess

   ⓒ correct as is

6. Brian bought <u>supply</u> for his trip.

   ⓐ supplys

   ⓑ supplies

   ⓒ correct as is

7. Miko saw a lark hopping among the <u>branchs</u> of a willow tree.

   ⓐ branches

   ⓑ branch

   ⓒ correct as is

8. All the <u>birds</u> scattered when Enrico jogged past a small bush.

   ⓐ birdes

   ⓑ bird

   ⓒ correct as is

9. She made two <u>wishs</u> before blowing out the candles on her birthday cake.

   ⓐ wishes

   ⓑ wish

   ⓒ correct as is

10. We have a few <u>holidays</u> this month when school will not be in session.

    ⓐ holiday

    ⓑ holidayes

    ⓒ correct as is

POSSESSIVE NOUNS

A. Underline the possessive noun in each sentence. On the line following each sentence, write *S* if the possessive noun is singular and *P* if it is plural.

1. Amelia's record flight across the Atlantic occurred in 1932. _____

2. During the Atlantic crossing, ice formed on the plane's wings. _____

3. Mexico's president greeted Amelia when she completed another flight from California to Mexico City. _____

4. Amelia Earhart was always interested in women's roles in aviation. _____

5. Men's career choices in aviation were more numerous at the time. _____

6. A university's financial support helped Amelia realize her dream of attempting a flight around the world. _____

B. Complete each sentence below using the possessive form of the noun in parentheses ( ).

1. The _____ runway was closed because of the storm. (airport)

2. We could see several _____ nests in the trees as our plane came in for a landing. (bird)

3. The _____ crew had to make quite a few preparations before the flight. (ship)

4. The two _____ attempts to land the planes were successful. (pilot)

5. The _____ luggage was collected by the ground crew and placed on a cart. (man)

6. The _____ coats were stored in an overhead bin on the airplane. (student)

POSSESSIVE NOUNS

A. Underline the possessive noun in each sentence. On the line following each sentence, write the word that names what the possessive noun owns.

1. Greenwood Elementary School's physical education program has been very successful during the past year. _____

2. The physical education teacher's records show that the students have excelled in many areas. _____

3. Many students were excited about Mrs. Rubowski's plans for physical education at Greenwood. _____

4. The teacher was ensuring that the Greenwood students met their state's physical fitness standards. _____

5. We're supposed to do twenty sit-ups by year's end. _____

6. John Davis's record for push-ups beat the previous record by four. _____

7. Yesterday, Lisa's speed in a race earned her a blue ribbon. _____

8. The students' overall performance ranked fifth in the state. _____

B. On the line, write the possessive form of each proper noun.

1. Chicago _____

2. Statue of Liberty _____

3. Yellowstone National Park _____

4. St. Louis _____

5. South Dakota _____

6. Mississippi River _____

POSSESSIVE NOUNS

A. Read each sentence. Then fill in the bubble next to the correct possessive form.

1. The ten explorer's equipment had been carefully selected and packed.

    ⓐ explorers

    ⓑ explorers'

    ⓒ correct as is

2. The journeys destination was the North Pole.

    ⓐ journey's

    ⓑ journeys'

    ⓒ correct as is

3. Two boats sailed through the region's icy water.

    ⓐ regions'

    ⓑ regions

    ⓒ correct as is

4. The two boats's designs enabled them to plow through thick ice floes.

    ⓐ boat's

    ⓑ boats'

    ⓒ correct as is

5. The explorers took photos for the Arctic Institutes's study group.

    ⓐ Arctic Institutes

    ⓑ Arctic Institute's

    ⓒ correct as is

6. A storms winds forced them to stop.

    ⓐ storm's

    ⓑ storms's

    ⓒ correct as is

7. The leader of the expedition began to worry about the groups food supply.

    ⓐ groups'

    ⓑ group's

    ⓒ correct as is

8. The next days' calm weather made everyone more confident.

    ⓐ day's

    ⓑ days's

    ⓒ correct as is

9. The womens' cabins were packed with flashlights and radios.

    ⓐ womens's

    ⓑ women's

    ⓒ correct as is

10. Dr. Lewis's journal detailed the progress of the expedition.

    ⓐ Dr. Lewis'

    ⓑ Dr. Lewi's

    ⓒ correct as is

ACTION VERBS WITH DIRECT OBJECTS

A. Underline the action verb in each sentence below.

1. One morning, Paul Bunyan's daughter Teeny took Slink for a walk.

2. Slink pushed a boulder down the path with his tail.

3. Teeny saw a large dead tree in the middle of the path.

4. Slink grabbed a huge branch off the tree.

5. Teeny observed the giant puma with amusement.

6. Then Teeny lifted the tree with just one hand.

7. She used it as a toothpick.

B. Complete each sentence with an action verb. The first one has been done for you.

1. Paul Bunyan _____discovered_____ the opening to a large cave one day.

2. Carrie _____ a huge cavern with her enormous ax.

3. Beautiful crystals _____ like thousands of lights.

4. Slink _____ his long tail.

5. The giant puma _____ syrup on Teeny's head.

6. Paul Bunyan _____ a hole out of the riverbed.

7. Ma and Pa _____ Teeny's hair in Niagara Falls.

8. The Bunyan family _____ across the country from coast to coast.

ACTION VERBS WITH DIRECT OBJECTS

A. Read each sentence below. Underline the action verb. Then circle the direct object.

1. Yvonne carried the groceries to the car.

2. Michael photographed many animals yesterday at the zoo.

3. I opened my present on the day before my birthday.

4. Lisa saw a turtle beside a rock in the pond.

5. I found the book on a shelf in my closet.

B. Complete each sentence below with a direct object that makes sense.

1. I found a _____ by the fountain in the park.

2. Jerry bought a _____ the day before he left on his trip.

3. Teresa made a _____ in art class yesterday.

4. Andy played the _____ at our school talent show.

5. Darlene took her _____ out of her locker before class.

C. Write two sentences, each with an action verb and a direct object. Underline the action verb and circle the direct object in your sentences.

1. _____

_____

2. _____

_____

ACTION VERBS WITH DIRECT OBJECTS

A. Fill in the bubble next to the direct object that appears in each sentence.

1. My brother collects baseball cards.
   - ⓐ baseball cards
   - ⓑ brother
   - ⓒ collects

2. Jan's dog chased the ball down the garden path.
   - ⓐ ball
   - ⓑ garden path
   - ⓒ dog

3. I prepared spaghetti for dinner this evening.
   - ⓐ dinner
   - ⓑ spaghetti
   - ⓒ I

4. Carlos gave his old bicycle to a friend.
   - ⓐ bicycle
   - ⓑ his
   - ⓒ friend

5. Should we take Willa to the park this afternoon?
   - ⓐ park
   - ⓑ we
   - ⓒ Willa

B. Read each sentence. Fill in the bubble next to the more vivid action verb.

1. The hungry dog quickly _____ its food.
   - ⓐ gobbled
   - ⓑ ate

2. The ferocious storm _____ a window in the old hotel.
   - ⓐ broke
   - ⓑ shattered

3. Matt _____ cold water after finishing the long, hot race.
   - ⓐ drank
   - ⓑ gulped

4. Donna _____ the map closely, looking for clues.
   - ⓐ studied
   - ⓑ read

5. She _____ the ball across the plate with lightning speed.
   - ⓐ threw
   - ⓑ hurled

VERB TENSES

A. Underline each verb. Write whether it is *present*, *past*, or *future*.

1. My friend Miles stopped by my house. _____

2. He is a serious computer whiz. _____

3. We chatted with some of our classmates on the Internet. _____

4. We also downloaded the lyrics to our favorite song. _____

5. I study the unusual rhymes in the lyrics. _____

6. Someday I will write great songs like that, too. _____

7. Later in the afternoon, we finished our homework together. _____

8. Tomorrow we will attend a concert. _____

B. Write each of the verbs from Part A in the correct column below. Then fill in the chart with the other tenses of that verb. The first one is done for you.

	Present Tense	Past Tense	Future Tense
1.	stop	stopped	will stop
2.			
3.			
4.			
5.			
6.			
7.			
8.			

VERB TENSES

The verbs in the following sentences are
underlined. Read each sentence.
Then write the tense *(past, present, future)*
of each verb on the line.

1. The family <u>arrived</u> in San Francisco.   _____

2. The boat <u>stopped</u> there.   _____

3. Soon the family <u>will drive</u> across the country.   _____

4. They <u>travel</u> for several days.   _____

5. The author's father <u>crosses</u> an old bridge.   _____

6. The car practically <u>raced</u> across the bridge.   _____

7. This action <u>scared</u> both mother and daughter.   _____

8. They <u>will remember</u> it forever!   _____

9. They <u>will hope</u> for no more similar events.   _____

10. The family <u>settled</u> in an overnight cabin.   _____

11. Jean and her mother <u>step</u> out of the car.   _____

12. They <u>see</u> so many new places.   _____

13. They <u>enjoyed</u> their stop in the Ozark Mountains.   _____

14. Jean <u>will reach</u> her grandparents' house soon.   _____

15. Everyone <u>greets</u> the family there.   _____

**On a separate piece of paper, write a paragraph that describes
how you felt about your home in the past, how you feel about it
right now, and how you will probably regard it in the future.**

VERB TENSES

A. Fill in the bubble that correctly identifies the tense of the underlined word or words.

1. My brother and I <u>explored</u> our new neighborhood today.

   ⓐ present
   ⓑ past
   ⓒ future

2. I really <u>like</u> the bicycle path along the main street.

   ⓐ present
   ⓑ past
   ⓒ future

3. We <u>asked</u> some kids about basketball courts in the area.

   ⓐ present
   ⓑ past
   ⓒ future

4. There <u>is</u> a nearby park with a swimming pool and basketball courts.

   ⓐ present
   ⓑ past
   ⓒ future

5. We <u>will spend</u> a lot of time there!

   ⓐ present
   ⓑ past
   ⓒ future

B. Fill in the bubble beside the verb that completes each sentence correctly.

1. I _____ the bus trip we took a week ago.

   ⓐ enjoy
   ⓑ will enjoy
   ⓒ enjoyed

2. My family and I _____ the Baseball Hall of Fame last weekend.

   ⓐ visit
   ⓑ visited
   ⓒ will visit

3. Last Saturday, we _____ a lot of new information about baseball.

   ⓐ learn
   ⓑ learned
   ⓒ will learn

4. In the years ahead, many new players _____ members of the Hall of Fame.

   ⓐ becomes
   ⓑ become
   ⓒ will become

5. Tomorrow I _____ my friend Pat to tell her about this fantastic trip.

   ⓐ will call
   ⓑ called
   ⓒ call

LINKING VERBS

A. Underline the verb in each sentence below. Then draw an arrow between the two words that the verb connects. The first one has been done for you.

1. The dog seemed upset by the storm.

2. Marcia's new kitten feels fluffy.

3. The cake in the bakery window looks delicious.

4. Ray's new CD player sounds terrific.

5. Sarah appeared relieved after the test.

B. Complete each sentence. Use one of the verbs from part A. Use each verb only once. The first one done for you.

1. After riding his bike all day, Marty _____appeared_____ tired.

2. That new movie I heard about last week _____ terrific.

3. Joanne _____ nervous just before the race.

4. Arthur _____ great in his new suit.

5. The new spring grass _____ soft under my feet.

C. Complete each sentence with a linking verb and a word that describes the subject.

1. John _____ _____ with his performance on the test.

2. The lamb's woolly coat _____ _____.

3. The new skyscraper downtown _____ _____.

4. Our school band _____ _____.

5. The squawking parrot _____ _____.

LINKING VERBS

am	was	look	taste
are	were	feel	smell
is	will	sound	seem

Read each sentence. Underline each linking verb. Then draw an arrow between the two words that it connects.

Example This adventure <u>was</u> risky.

1. I am curious about Ernest Shackleton.

2. His life sounds interesting.

3. Shackleton's Antarctic adventure was dangerous.

4. Still, the men seemed cheerful through it all.

5. The photographs in the selection are fascinating.

6. You almost feel the bitter cold.

7. Here are some facts I learned.

8. Seal meat tastes oily.

9. The sea smells salty.

10. Antarctica looks lonely.

Work with a partner to write a description of Antarctica or of one adventure Shackleton and his men experienced. Use linking verbs.

LINKING VERBS

A. Fill in the bubble next to the linking verb that is in each sentence.

1. The soda in the refrigerator is very cold.

ⓐ is

ⓑ in

ⓒ very

2. Rose seems confident on the pitcher's mound.

ⓐ confident

ⓑ Rose

ⓒ seems

3. The air feels warm this beautiful spring morning.

ⓐ this

ⓑ warm

ⓒ feels

4. The violent storm appears to be over now.

ⓐ appears

ⓑ storm

ⓒ over

5. Stuart was bored and restless during the long movie.

ⓐ restless

ⓑ was

ⓒ during

B. Fill in the bubble next to the linking verb that correctly completes each sentence.

1. There _____ a concert in the park tomorrow afternoon.

ⓐ will be

ⓑ was

ⓒ has been

2. I _____ certain that the mayor will attend our play.

ⓐ are

ⓑ am

ⓒ were

3. The thunderstorm _____ very loud last night.

ⓐ will be

ⓑ is

ⓒ was

4. That exhibit _____ postponed.

ⓐ has been

ⓑ were

ⓒ had

5. The batter at the plate _____ eager to score a run.

ⓐ were

ⓑ seems

ⓒ am

Name

MAIN AND HELPING VERBS

RETEACHING: A **main verb** shows the action or state of being in a sentence. A **helping verb** such as *am, are, has, have, had,* or *will* works with the main verb to show when the action or state of being occurs.

A. In each sentence, underline the main verb twice and the helping verb once.

1. I am studying the amazing life of Wilma Rudolph.

2. My class will write reports about this sports legend.

3. We have read an exciting account of her triumphs.

4. Teresa is painting a picture of the famous runner.

5. Matthew and I are working on a poster about Wilma's victories.

6. Wilma had overcome serious physical problems.

7. Her mother had given her a great deal of support.

8. The people in Wilma's hometown were cheering for her.

9. People will remember Wilma Rudolph's accomplishments for many years.

10. Her story has inspired young athletes around the world.

B. Use one of the helping verbs in the box to complete each sentence. Then underline the main verb in each sentence twice. One helping verb will be used more than once.

am	are	is	will

1. I _____ reading a book about Wilma Rudolph's determination.

2. Wilma _____ practicing exercises for her leg.

3. She and her mother _____ traveling to the nearest hospital.

4. In spite of the difficulties, Wilma _____ fight back.

5. I _____ rooting for Wilma to succeed.

MAIN AND HELPING VERBS

Read the sentences below. Underline the main verbs and write the helping verbs on the lines provided.

1. Wilma had weighed only four pounds at birth. _____

2. Others have expected little from her. _____

3. She is becoming a great athlete. _____

4. Not a single problem has stopped her. _____

5. People are noticing her skill in basketball. _____

6. Wilma will surprise everyone. _____

7. They are urging her to run races. _____

8. The sweat is flying off her face. _____

9. She has lunged across the finish line. _____

10. She is not thinking about her fear or pain. _____

11. She was forgetting all her problems. _____

12. People in the crowd were cheering for her. _____

13. No American woman had captured three gold medals at one Olympics. _____

14. She has changed sports history. _____

15. We will tell others about Wilma Rudolph's accomplishments. _____

Imagine that you were at the Olympics on the day that Wilma Rudolph won three gold medals. Write a paragraph describing the reaction of the crowd. What were people doing, thinking, and feeling? Use main and helping verbs in your writing.

MAIN AND HELPING VERBS

Fill in the bubble next to the helping verb that correctly completes each sentence.

1. Lily, Frank, and I _____ joining a neighborhood swimming team.

   ⓐ am
   ⓑ is
   ⓒ are

2. I _____ thought about joining the team for a couple of months.

   ⓐ was
   ⓑ had
   ⓒ has

3. Frank _____ taken diving lessons at a YMCA indoor pool.

   ⓐ has
   ⓑ have
   ⓒ is

4. We _____ practiced a great deal.

   ⓐ will
   ⓑ has
   ⓒ have

5. The team's coach _____ analyzing everyone's strengths and weaknesses.

   ⓐ is
   ⓑ are
   ⓒ have

6. The coach _____ post the results on the bulletin board in two weeks.

   ⓐ will
   ⓑ have
   ⓒ had

7. Our team's season _____ not begun.

   ⓐ is
   ⓑ have
   ⓒ has

8. Our team _____ probably compete with other teams from the area.

   ⓐ have
   ⓑ had
   ⓒ will

9. We _____ going with my mother to a sports equipment store tomorrow.

   ⓐ was
   ⓑ are
   ⓒ is

10. I _____ outgrown the swimsuit I wore last summer.

    ⓐ have
    ⓑ was
    ⓒ will

IRREGULAR VERBS

A. On the line, write the past tense or the past participle form of the verb in parentheses ( ).

1. I _____ I lost my math book. (think)

2. My friend had _____ a fancy seashell. (find)

3. Ed _____ his new CD to my house. (bring)

4. Have you _____ the new coach? (meet)

5. She _____ she would get the team in shape. (say)

6. My neighbors _____ me for baby-sitting. (pay)

7. John _____ the football. (catch)

8. The little boy _____ his balloon tightly. (hold)

9. I have _____ about learning a new sport. (think)

10. The first night, I _____ the new puppy in my room. (keep)

11. Denise _____ a gold locket in the park the other day. (find)

12. We have already _____ for our tickets. (pay)

13. My sister has _____ a cold. (catch)

14. Maya has _____ a journal for many years. (keep)

15. Steve and I _____ in first grade. (meet)

B. Use each of the following verbs in a sentence.

     write   wrote   have written

1. _____

2. _____

3. _____

IRREGULAR VERBS

Read each sentence. On the line, write the
past tense or past participle form of the verb
in parentheses.

1. They had _____ home to America. (come)

2. They _____ about their trip across the ocean. (speak)

3. They _____ many things to do. (find)

4. They _____ and danced on the ship. (sing)

5. They _____ pictures, too. (take)

6. Jean Fritz has _____ about the journey. (write)

7. She has _____ some good moments to retell. (chose)

8. Some events are _____ in her memory. (freeze)

9. Time has not _____ them from her. (steal)

10. She _____ her first sight of America very exciting. (find)

11. She _____ a glimpse of the Hawaiian Islands. (catch)

12. She has never _____ sight of them in her memory. (lose)

13. Lines of poetry _____ from her lips. (spring)

14. Many people have _____ this is a good story. (say)

15. Jean Fritz has _____ a reputation as a good author. (build)

 On a separate piece of paper, write about an exciting adventure in your
own past. Use at least one past tense form and one past participle form.

IRREGULAR VERBS

Choose the verb form that correctly completes each sentence.
Fill in the bubble next to your answer.

1. My friend Alex _____ several National Parks.

   ⓐ see
   ⓑ has saw
   ⓒ has seen

2. He _____ an arrowhead in Montana.

   ⓐ find
   ⓑ has find
   ⓒ found

3. In Colorado, he _____ a real dinosaur fossil in his hand.

   ⓐ held
   ⓑ hold
   ⓒ has hold

4. He _____ a visit to Abraham Lincoln's birthplace in Kentucky.

   ⓐ pay
   ⓑ paid
   ⓒ has pay

5. He was on Assateague Island when wild ponies _____ ashore.

   ⓐ swims
   ⓑ swam
   ⓒ has swum

6. I _____ him that next time I would go with him.

   ⓐ tells
   ⓑ has told
   ⓒ told

7. Once I _____ home shells from the ocean.

   ⓐ brings
   ⓑ has bring
   ⓒ brought

8. I _____ many souvenirs from the trips I have taken.

   ⓐ have kept
   ⓑ has kept
   ⓒ keeps

9. Where were you when the bell _____?

   ⓐ ring
   ⓑ rang
   ⓒ rings

10. Oh no, I _____ my souvenir!

   ⓐ has broke
   ⓑ have broken
   ⓒ breaks

PRONOUNS

RETEACHING: A **pronoun** is a word that takes the place of a noun or nouns. Pronouns show number. They indicate one or more than one.

A. Underline the pronoun in each sentence. Then circle the word or words to which the pronoun refers.

1. Savannah and Elana agreed to eat lunch together. They decided to meet at noon.

2. "Which train should I take?" David wondered, studying the train schedule.

3. Melanie opened the door. She was surprised when people shouted, "Happy birthday!"

4. The barn might look deserted, but it has become a home to many birds.

5. Frank has already eaten half of the bread he baked this afternoon.

B. Read each sentence pair. Underline the pronouns. On the lines, write the pronouns and the nouns they replace. The first one is an example.

1. Joe bought a gift last week. He gave it to Margarita yesterday.

   He = Joe   it = gift

2. Many people are in line, waiting to buy this book. They have been waiting to buy it all afternoon.

   _____   _____

3. Amy and Duncan paddled the canoe upriver for three hours. "We have been paddling all afternoon," said Amy, "and I am getting tired."

   _____   _____

4. Did Emma get the eggs? She will need them for dinner.

   _____   _____

PRONOUNS

Read the sentences. Write a pronoun on the line that could take the place of the underlined words.

1. <u>Talent shows</u> can make people nervous. _____

2. <u>A talent show</u> gives people a chance to show off. _____

3. <u>My younger brother</u> was in the talent show at my school. _____

4. Lots of people clapped loudly for <u>my brother</u>. _____

5. <u>My older sister</u> did not want to be in the show. _____

6. I did not blame <u>my older sister</u>. _____

7. I was nervous about being in <u>the talent show</u>, too. _____

8. <u>Pam, Alicia, and I</u> decided to sing a round. _____

9. People clapped politely for <u>Pam, Alicia, and me</u>. _____

10. We thanked <u>the audience members</u> for applauding. _____

11. You can ask <u>Mrs. Renko</u> about how well we did! _____

12. Now <u>my sister</u> is thinking about being in a show. _____

13. I asked <u>my parents</u> if my brother, sister, and I could practice at home. _____

14. Next year, <u>the talent show</u> will be even better! _____

Imagine that you are dancing or singing in a talent show and the music suddenly stops or begins to skip. On a separate piece of paper, write two or three sentences telling how you feel and how others react. Underline all the pronouns that you use.

PRONOUNS

A. Fill in the bubble next to the pronoun that correctly replaces the underlined words in each sentence.

1. Lou picked some flowers in the garden and put <u>the flowers</u> in a vase.

   ⓐ it

   ⓑ them

   ⓒ her

2. Don't buy those shoes if <u>the shoes</u> don't feel comfortable.

   ⓐ it

   ⓑ I

   ⓒ they

3. Sarah said <u>Sarah</u> would help wash the car today.

   ⓐ I

   ⓑ we

   ⓒ she

4. Mel made a surprise dinner for <u>Laura</u>.

   ⓐ her

   ⓑ him

   ⓒ them

5. Will played a great game, and everyone patted <u>Will</u> on the back.

   ⓐ them

   ⓑ him

   ⓒ us

B. Fill in the bubble next to the pronoun that correctly completes each sentence.

1. Cindy, Jon, and I decided that _____ would all meet after school.

   ⓐ we

   ⓑ he

   ⓒ she

2. The ball flew overhead, and then _____ disappeared into the trees.

   ⓐ it

   ⓑ they

   ⓒ we

3. Leo told all nine of _____ the news.

   ⓐ me

   ⓑ him

   ⓒ us

4. I thanked my parents for the present they gave _____.

   ⓐ it

   ⓑ me

   ⓒ them

5. The coach said, "_____ am sure we'll win!"

   ⓐ we

   ⓑ I

   ⓒ me

SUBJECT AND OBJECT PRONOUNS

A. Read the sentence pairs below. Underline the pronoun in the second sentence. Then circle the noun it replaces in the first sentence.

1. The woodcutter saw a neighbor working in the garden. The woodcutter approached him.

2. "Those roses are beautiful," said the woodcutter. "They have a wonderful scent."

3. "This garden is a joy," said the woodcutter's neighbor. "It gets a lot of sun."

4. "There's an easier way to dig holes," said the woodcutter. "A shovel could dig them in half the time."

5. The neighbor just smiled at the woodcutter and said, "Good day to you, sir."

6. The woodcutter shrugged. Then he walked away.

B. Underline all pronouns in each sentence below. Then, above each one, write *S* if it is a subject pronoun, or *O* if it is an object pronoun.

1. The woodcutter's wife asked him to go to the woods.

2. "I want you to chop some wood," she said.

3. "We have guests coming to visit us," said the woodcutter's wife.

4. "They will be here soon. Let's serve them dinner," his wife continued.

5. The woodcutter found an ax, and he picked it up.

6. "I will be back in a jiffy," the woodcutter told her.

7. "I will be here," the wife answered. "Don't make me wait too long."

Name _____

SUBJECT AND OBJECT PRONOUNS

In each sentence, circle the correct pronoun in parentheses ( ).

1. The woodcutter's wife warns (he, him).

2. The woodcutter does not hear (she, her).

3. The woodcutter and (she, her) often ignore each other.

4. (They, Them) do not see eye to eye.

5. The woodcutter just watched (them, they).

6. Amy and (I, me) felt sorry for the woodcutter.

7. (Us, We) might have done the same thing.

8. (He, Him) did not seem like such an unlikeable character.

9. We told Katie and (she, her) about this story.

10. (They, Them) had different ideas about the story.

11. Matt wanted Katie and (I, me) to agree with him.

12. We asked (he, him) to explain his ideas.

13. Then he told Katie and (I, me) his opinion.

14. The opinions were different. We couldn't change (they, them)!

15. (He, him), Katie, and I will have to read it again.

Why don't some people listen to good advice? On a separate piece of paper, write two or three sentences explaining why this might be so. Use as many subject and object pronouns as possible.

SUBJECT AND OBJECT PRONOUNS

A. Fill in the bubble next to the pronoun that correctly completes each sentence.

1. _____ will all meet at my house after the game.

   (a) We
   (b) Them
   (c) Us

2. _____ decided to hold a meeting tomorrow after school.

   (a) Us
   (b) Them
   (c) They

3. Lydia and _____ are going to be in the play.

   (a) me
   (b) I
   (c) us

4. Bruce met _____ at the football game.

   (a) we
   (b) I
   (c) me

5. Jeff bought a used bike and painted _____ red.

   (a) it
   (b) him
   (c) them

B. Decide if the underlined part of each sentence is correct. Fill in the bubble next to the right answer.

1. They tried out for the basketball team.

   (a) Them
   (b) Us
   (c) correct as is

2. Susan promised to take they to the lake tomorrow.

   (a) them
   (b) we
   (c) correct as is

3. Dad took I and Mark to the beach today.

   (a) Mark and I
   (b) Mark and me
   (c) correct as is

4. Her and me have been friends for a long time.

   (a) Me and she
   (b) She and I
   (c) correct as is

5. Me and him are exactly the same age.

   (a) He and I
   (b) Him and me
   (c) correct as is

POSSESSIVE PRONOUNS

A. Circle the possessive pronoun in each sentence. Then draw an arrow to the noun that it describes.

1. My family is moving next summer, so we're cleaning out the house.

2. You wouldn't believe what we found in our attic!

3. Mom and Dad discovered a stack of old photos from their honeymoon.

4. Ella found her first bicycle.

5. Adam found his diary from third grade.

6. Now he is looking for its key.

7. What do you think you would find in your house?

B. Write the possessive pronoun that goes with each subject pronoun.

1. I _____   4. she _____   6. we _____

2. you _____   5. it _____   7. they _____

3. he _____

C. Choose three pairs of pronouns from the list above. Then write a sentence using each pair.

1.

2. _____

3. _____

POSSESSIVE PRONOUNS

**A. Circle the pronoun in parentheses ( )
that correctly completes each sentence.**

1. They practiced (their / theirs) lines over
   and over again.

2. She uses (her / hers) talent to create beautiful
   heroines.

3. "Is that (my / mine) playbook?" asked Lily.

4. "No! It is (my / mine)," replied Sean.

5. The play is about a woman's struggle to find (her / hers) missing sister.

**B. Rewrite the sentences, using possessive pronouns in place of the
underlined words.**

1. Which dresses in the closet are <u>Barbara's</u>?

   _____

2. This is <u>Ken and Tony's</u> collection of dried flowers.

   _____

3. I am enjoying <u>Paul's</u> book.

   _____

4. <u>Elizabeth's</u> disappointment showed clearly.

   _____

5. Is this <u>Kevin's</u> idea of a joke?

   _____

**Cut out a newspaper or magazine article.
Underline all the possessive pronouns.**

POSSESSIVE PRONOUNS

A. Fill in the bubble next to the pronoun that correctly completes each sentence.

1. Every night, the older children on _____ block get together.

   ⓐ mine
   ⓑ my
   ⓒ ours

2. If Lila is there, we play basketball at _____ house.

   ⓐ her
   ⓑ hers
   ⓒ its

3. When Ray and Maria are home, we play at _____.

   ⓐ its
   ⓑ theirs
   ⓒ their

4. Tonight, Al and Rob are bringing _____ soccer ball.

   ⓐ his
   ⓑ theirs
   ⓒ their

5. Tomorrow night, I will bring _____.

   ⓐ mine
   ⓑ my
   ⓒ our

B. Decide which pronoun correctly replaces the underlined words. Fill in the bubble next to your answer.

1. Mr. and Mrs. Espy's daughter Tracy won a trophy for soccer.

   ⓐ Theirs
   ⓑ Their
   ⓒ Her

2. "This Year's Most Valuable Player" is written on the trophy's base.

   ⓐ my
   ⓑ its
   ⓒ her

3. Tracy's team will play in the State Championship.

   ⓐ Our
   ⓑ Her
   ⓒ Hers

4. Last year, Alan's school won the championship.

   ⓐ him
   ⓑ his
   ⓒ its

5. This year, victory will be Tracy's.

   ⓐ her
   ⓑ theirs
   ⓒ hers

SUBJECT-VERB AGREEMENT

A. Draw one line under the subject in each sentence. Draw two lines under the verb. Then write *S* if the subject and verb are singular or *P* if they are plural.

1. A conductor beats time with a baton. _____

2. Many musicians memorize their music. _____

3. The principal violinist leads the other musicians. _____

4. The concert hall buzzes with voices. _____

5. Mariachi bands consist of violins, guitars, trumpets, and singers. _____

6. The singers and lead guitarist often practice together. _____

7. Jazz groups perform at the State Theater in our city. _____

8. A pianist works hard to prepare for a performance. _____

B. Write the present tense form of the verb in parentheses ( ) that correctly completes each sentence.

1. Mariachi bands _____ all over the world. (play)

2. My cousin _____ everywhere with the band. (go)

3. The trumpet player always _____ a radio with him. (take)

4. The guitarist in this band also _____ music. (write)

5. The drummer _____ the conductor carefully. (watch)

6. My favorite singer _____ two songs on the Top Ten list. (have)

7. My brother and I _____ to them every morning. (listen)

8. Jamal and Denise _____ the city every year. (visit)

SUBJECT-VERB AGREEMENT

A. Write the correct present tense form of the verb in parentheses ( ) to complete each sentence.

1. Advertisements sometimes _____ people to buy things they don't need. (persuade)

2. Wendy usually _____ at the library on Saturday. (study)

3. Please _____ the missing locket. (describe)

4. When the cat _____, I will take good care of it. (arrive)

5. No one ever _____ the clock in our class. (watch)

6. I write to him often, but he seldom _____. (reply)

7. Mr. Swanson _____ landscapes on Sunday afternoons. (paint)

8. He _____ to San Francisco tomorrow. (fly)

9. The races _____ at Barrow Street. (end)

10. Mary and Denise always _____ school baseball games. (attend)

B. Complete each sentence using a present tense action verb.

1. My friends and I _____ on Saturdays.

2. Jeff _____ every summer.

3. Anna always _____ on the weekend.

C. Write one sentence describing your best friend and another sentence about someplace you like to go together. Use present tense verbs in both sentences.

1. _____

2. _____

DIALOGUE AND QUOTATIONS

A. In each sentence, underline the words that the speaker or speakers actually said. Then add quotation marks where they belong.

1. Can't we stay up just five more minutes? the children begged.

2. Shoo Kate replied, That's another story.

3. What's for lunch? Bob asked.

4. I am so excited! Betsy cried.

B. The following dialogue is missing commas, question marks, and other necessary punctuation. Write the correct punctuation on each line.

1. Poissant said__ "I remember once when Duke Ellington stayed at my house__"

2. "Was Duke Ellington famous__" Punkin asked__

3. "He sure was__" Miss Ida exclaimed__

4. "I not only met him__" Poissant explained__ "but I was sitting in the parlor when he sat down at the piano and started to play__"

C. All the punctuation, including quotation marks, is missing from this dialogue. Write the missing punctuation marks on the lines.

1. __Duke's playing sure heated up that little room__ __ exclaimed Poissant__

2. __Did any other famous people stay at your house__ __ asked Freda__

3. __No__ __ said Poissant__ __but Lena Horne once stayed at Miss Jackson's house__ __

4. Then he added__ __However__ that is a story for another day__ __

DIALOGUE AND QUOTATIONS

RETEACHING: Quotation marks are used to show the beginning and end of someone's exact words. An **indirect quotation** is a summary of what someone has written or said. Quotation marks are not used in indirect quotations.

A. Write *direct* next to the direct quotation, which shows the speaker's exact words. Write *indirect* next to the indirect quotation.

1 **a.** "I have a dream," Martin Luther King, Jr., stated. _____

  b. Martin Luther King, Jr., said that he had a dream. _____

2 **a.** Aesop said that kindness is never wasted. _____

  b. "No act of kindness is ever wasted," said Aesop. _____

B. Add punctuation to these direct quotations. Be sure to capitalize proper names and words at the beginning of sentences. Use the proofreading mark (≡) for a capital letter.

1. Franklin Delano Roosevelt stated, the only thing we have to fear is fear itself

2. You must do the thing you think you cannot do Eleanor Roosevelt advised.

3. whoever is happy will make others happy Anne Frank wrote

4. If winter comes, can spring be far behind asked the poet Shelley

5. Mark Twain joked everyone talks about the weather, but no one does anything about it

C. Rewrite each indirect quotation as a direct quotation.

1. I told my friends that I was glad they came.

_____

2. John asked me what I thought of the movie.

_____

ADJECTIVES

A. Complete the following phrases. For 1–4, write an adjective. For 5–8, write the article *a* or *an* and a noun.

1. a _____ game

2. a _____ street

3. an _____ book

4. an _____ dog

5. _____ incredible _____

6. _____ beautiful _____

7. _____ exciting _____

8. _____ colorful _____

B. In each sentence, underline each adjective and circle the noun that it describes.

1. Alice visited an interesting museum.

2. The museum was filled with fascinating art.

3. The guide provided detailed descriptions.

4. The bronze statue was her favorite.

5. One entire floor was devoted to bright paintings of blue flowers.

6. The top floor contained ten enormous sculptures.

7. The museum is a popular tourist stop.

8. Visitors can buy a delicious lunch in the cafeteria.

9. Beautiful gifts are sold in the shop.

10. Many visitors spend a full day in the museum.

PREPOSITIONS

A. Complete each sentence with one of the prepositional phrases. Use each phrase only once. Then write whether the phrase tells where or when something took place.

during the summer	in the afternoon	in the ocean
to the neighborhood pool	in Nebraska	

1. My family and I live _____. _____

2. Swimming is my favorite thing to do _____. _____

3. My friends and I can walk _____. _____

4. Sometimes _____ we take our cousins. _____

5. My friend, who lives in Miami, swims _____. _____

B. In each sentence, circle the prepositional phrase and underline the preposition.

1. Gerard is giving a party for Maria.

2. Norma sent invitations to all their friends.

3. The food was made by Josue.

4. Rebecca decorated the room with streamers.

5. Mela sat next to Danielle.

6. Kama played a song on her guitar.

7. Terry arrived late with Deborah.

8. Adriane brought a huge chocolate cake from the bakery.

9. The celebration lasted until dinnertime.

10. Sarah and Joanna took the train home with Liza.

ADVERBS

RETEACHING: An **adverb** is a word that describes a verb, an adjective, or another adverb. Some adverbs tell when or where something happens.

A. Complete the chart by writing the comparative and superlative form of each adverb. Use *more* or *most*. Then complete each sentence with a comparison, using an adverb from the chart.

Adverb	Comparative Adverb	Superlative Adverb
slowly		
gracefully		
fiercely		
swiftly		

1. A dolphin swims _____

2. A turtle moves _____

3. Tyrannosaurus rex roared _____

B. In each sentence, underline the adverb and circle the verb it describes.

1. Anna jumped quickly into the pool.

2. Danny sat quietly on the sidelines.

3. The dog gently pushed open the door.

4. The animal waited patiently to be fed.

5. Laurie tenderly petted the puppy.

6. The crowd cheered loudly when the team scored a goal.

7. Joseph told him later about the party.

8. Lucy immediately volunteered to make invitations.

9. The cat boldly climbed the tree.

COMMAS AND COLONS

A. Answer the questions, paying careful attention to your use of commas and colons.

1. Write your name and the names of two classmates as they would appear on an official document.

   _____

   _____

   _____

2. What is your date of birth? _____

3. What time does your school begin? _____ end? _____

B. Read each sentence. Add a comma or colon where needed. Write *correct* if the sentence is correct.

1. Luke Sam and Nick are putting on a play.

2. The play will begin at 800 PM.

3. Yalixa his sister wrote the play.

4. They will perform the play Wednesday and Thursday.

5. Amy can you make the costumes?

6. Like her mom Luisa is a good singer.

7. Our flag is red white and blue.

8. Michael plays baseball and soccer.

9. Nathan will visit on March 28 2004.

10. We are always happy when he comes but sad when he leaves.

RETEACHING: **Diagramming** a sentence shows how all the words in the sentence work together.

DIAGRAMMING SENTENCES

A. Underline the articles and adjectives in each sentence. Circle any adverbs. Then diagram each sentence. The model diagram will help you.

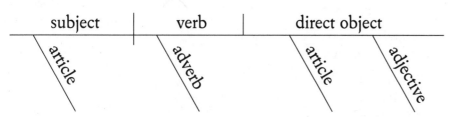

1. The dancer made a graceful movement.

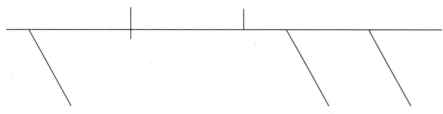

2. The tiny cricket slowly ate the green leaf.

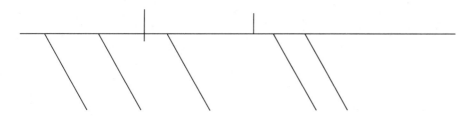

B. Complete the diagram for the following sentence.

1. The playful kitten gleefully chased the red ball.

Page 5

A. 1. interrogative   4. imperative
2. exclamatory   5. declarative
3. declarative   6. exclamatory

B. 1. incomplete   3. incomplete
2. complete   4. complete

C. 1. I ate the salad with my fork.
2. My mother was proud of my award.

Page 6

A. 1. Do you like to write poems?   interrogative
2. I can't believe my story won!   exclamatory
3. He asked me a lot of questions.   declarative
4. Write back to me soon.   imperative

B. Answers will vary.

Page 7

1. b   3. b   5. a   7. b   9. c
2. a   4. c   6. c   8. a   10. a

Page 8

A. 1. This story | tells about Jamie and Grama Bowman.
2. Grama Bowman | used to tell Jamie stories.
3. Jamie's great-grandmother | loved to see the fox's tracks.
4. Her best friend, Wokwses the Fox, | left the tracks.
5. That clever fox | delighted Grama.
6. Grama's song | is a kind of fox song.

B. 1. The autumn leaves were blowing in the wind.
2. The old Indian people told a story about the leaves.
3. The fall season is the time for leaf dances.
4. The leaves put on their best colors at that time.
5. The cold, autumn wind comes to take them.
6. Grama Bowman, a wise woman, told Jamie this.
7. The old leaves are like old people.
8. Their final dances are very beautiful.
9. The very best dances occur in autumn.
10. Grama Bowman's story explains a natural event.

Page 9

A. 1. Old, wise Grama Bowman teaches Jamie a song.
2. The first line of the song is "Hey, kwah nu deh."
3. The words of the song repeat.
4. This song, a kind of chant, stays in Jamie's memory forever.
5. Her dream includes this song.
6. A fox with glistening eyes appears in the answer to the song.
7. The fox, a mysterious animal, disappears again.

B. 1. The events in Jamie's dream tell a great deal.
2. Her conversations in the dream show her relationship to Grama Bowman.
3. Their actions reveal a loving closeness.
4. Jamie, Grama Bowman's great granddaughter, learns from her.
5. Both characters enjoy each other's company.
6. Grama's lessons to her will live on in Jamie's memory.
7. Grama Bowman, a guide and teacher, shares her knowledge.
8. The world of nature is Grama's home.

Page 10

A. 1. a   2. c   3. b   4. c   5. b
B. 1. a   2. c   3. c   4. b   5. a

Page 11

A. 1. Listening to the radio is popular among my classmates. B
2. My friends and I listen to the latest pop music on the radio. A
3. Our class danced in the gym last Friday afternoon. A
4. Some of the teachers at the dance sang some "oldies." A
5. The dance was a huge success among students and teachers. B
6. Some parents stood along the side of the gym. A
7. They seemed amused by the music and dancing. B

B. Answers will vary.

Page 12

A. 1. The game against the Kansas City Royals would start soon.
2. The left fielder was running out to the field beside Ken.
3. A tingle of excitement went down Ken junior's back.
4. The new left fielder was none other than his dad.
5. The crowd at the stadium let out a roar.
6. All the fans, in the stadium and out of it, knew this was a great moment.
7. Ken, the left fielder's son, felt so happy!

B. 1. I read the story of Ken Griffey, Junior and Senior.
2. These two famous players are father and son.
3. They even played on the same team together.
4. Both men were in the Seattle Mariners line-up.
5. This father-son team made history.
6. The president of the United States sent them a telegram after one great game.
7. The Griffeys appeared together on a few television shows.
8. These two great athletes remain famous today.

Page 13

A. 1. b   2. a   3. b   4. c   5. a
B. 1. b   2. a   3. c   4. a   5. c

Page 14

A. 1. Families and friends often help each other during times of hardship.
2. During a war, people sometimes leave their homes and lose their belongings.
3. Intelligence, courage, and luck can help people survive.
4. Food and clean water may become scarce.
5. Many young people join the army or work in factories.

B. 1. Annemarie and Ellen played with the dolls.
2. Kirsti cried and complained about the shoes.
3. Annemarie brushed her hair and handed the brush to Ellen.
4. Families hid in the house or fled to the forest.

Page 15

A. 1. Annemarie and Ellen are good friends.
2. Their homes and families are in Denmark.
3. The girls sometimes talk or giggle with Annemarie's sister.
4. All three children joke, laugh, and play games together.
5. The Rosens or the Johansens will be there.
6. Families and friends help each other in time of war.
7. The Johansens hide Ellen and keep her safe.
8. Ellen reads and sings to Kirsti.
9. Denmark, Holland, and other countries struggled during the war.
10. People succeed or fail in surprising ways.

B. Answers will vary.

Page 16

1. b   3. c   5. a   7. a   9. b
2. c   4. b   6. a   8. a   10. c

Page 17

A. 1. I want to go to the movies, but my friend Pat does not.
2. It rained last night, and we had to stay home.
3. Ed will drive to Texas, or he will take the train.
4. It snowed this morning, but the sun came out this afternoon.

B. 1. We wanted to ride our bikes home, but mine had a flat tire.
2. The whistle blew, and the train pulled out of the station.
3. I will finish the job today, or Bob will finish it tomorrow.

Page 18

A. 1. Our cousins arrived, and we were very happy to see them.
2. Eileen had cut her hair short, but her twin sister Emily still had long hair.
3. They had always looked exactly alike, and I could not get used to them.
4. Would they play with me, or would they play only with my older sisters?
5. First Eileen gave me a hug, and then Emily did the same.
6. Our parents went into the kitchen to talk, but the rest of us preferred to be outside.
7. We used to have a hiding place, but I was not sure if Eileen and Emily would remember it.
8. At dinner, Mom said the twins could stay with us, or we could go stay with them.

Page 19

1. b   3. a   5. c   7. a   9. a
2. c   4. a   6. b   8. c   10. b

Page 20

A. 1. Mr. Sherlock Holmes is a famous fictional detective.
2. This character was created by the author Sir Arthur Conan Doyle.
3. Holmes appeared in 56 stories and several novels written by Doyle, including *The Sign of Four*.
4. He was often assisted by his friend Dr. John Watson.
5. They worked together on mysteries throughout the city of London.

B. 1. proper, common, proper
2. proper, common
3. common, proper
4. common, common, common
5. proper, proper, common

Page 21

A. 1. I read the (Dallas Morning News) every day. newspaper
2. We have two dogs, named (Archie) and (Samantha.) pet names
3. In the fall, I will attend (Nichols Middle School.) school
4. We are going to read about the (Industrial Revolution.) historical era
5. Did you have a good time at our (Fourth of July) picnic this year? holiday
6. I want to join the (National Geographic Society) organization

B. Some answers will vary.
Common noun: city, holiday, business
Proper noun: Ice Age, Rover, George Washington

Page 22

1. a   3. b   5. a   7. a   9. a
2. c   4. b   6. c   8. b   10. c

Page 23

A. 1. (park), pictures
2. photographs, (camera), (bench)
3. (rabbit), bushes, birds, branches, (head)
4. strangers, (path)
5. notes, (foot)
6. (paper), (code)
7. (case), members, (agency)

B. 1. Ricardo snapped on the lights and studied the coded messages.
2. Vikki gave him the snapshots of the suspects.
3. He was carrying his newspapers and his suitcases.

Page 24

A. 1. ride   3. town   5. moon
2. route   4. tree   6. trip

B. 1. classes   3. libraries   5. benches
2. buildings   4. churches   6. cities

Page 25

1. a   3. a   5. c   7. a   9. a
2. c   4. b   6. b   8. c   10. c

Page 26

A. 1. Amelia's, S   3. Mexico's, S   5. Men's, P
2. plane's, S   4. women's, P   6. university's, S

B. 1. airport's   3. ship's   5. man's
2. birds'   4. pilots'   6. students'

Page 27

A. 1. School's program   5. year's end
2. teacher's records   6. Davis's record
3. Mrs. Rubowski's plans   7. Lisa's speed
4. state's standards   8. students' performance

B. 1. Chicago's   4. St. Louis's
2. Statue of Liberty's   5. South Dakota's
3. Yellowstone National Park's   6. Mississippi River's

Page 28

1. b   3. c   5. b   7. b   9. b
2. a   4. b   6. a   8. a   10. c

Page 29

A. 1. took   3. saw   5. observed   7. used
2. pushed   4. grabbed   6. lifted

B. Sample answers are given.
1. discovered   5. dumped, spilled
2. made, hammered, dug   6. scooped, dug
3. sparkled, glittered, shone   7. washed, scrubbed
4. flicked, swished, moved   8. walked, traveled

Page 30

A. 1. carried, (groceries)   4. saw, (turtle)
2. photographed, (animals)   5. found, (book)
3. opened, (present)

B. Answers will vary.
C. Answers will vary.

Page 31

A. 1. a   2. a   3. b   4. a   5. c
B. 1. a   2. b   3. b   4. a   5. b

Page 32

A. 1. stopped, past   5. study, present
2. is, present   6. will write, future
3. chatted, past   7. finished, past
4. downloaded, past   8. will attend, future

B. 2. is, was, will be
3. chat, chatted, will chat
4. download, downloaded, will download
5. study, studied, will study
6. write, wrote, will write
7. finish, finished, will finish
8. attend, attended, will attend

Page 33

1. past   6. past   11. present
2. past   7. past   12. present
3. future   8. future   13. past
4. present   9. future   14. future
5. present   10. past   15. present

Page 34

A. 1. b   2. a   3. b   4. a   5. c
B. 1. c   2. b   3. b   4. c   5. a

Page 35

A. 1. dog seemed upset   4. player sounds terrific.
2. kitten feels fluffy   5. Sarah appeared relieved
3. cake in the bakery window looks delicious.

B. Answers may vary.
1. appeared   3. seemed   5. feels
2. sounds   4. looks

C. Sample answers given.
1. was, pleased   3. looks, beautiful   5. seems, angry
2. feels, soft   4. sounds, great

Page 36

1. I am curious
2. life sounds interesting
3. adventure was dangerous.
4. men seemed cheerful
5. photographs in the selection are fascinating
6. You almost feel the bitter cold.
7. Here are some facts
8. meat tastes oily.
9. sea smells salty.
10. Antarctica looks lonely.

Page 37

A. 1. a   2. c   3. c   4. a   5. b
B. 1. a   2. b   3. c   4. a   5. b

Page 38

A. 1. am studying   6. had overcome
2. will write   7. had given
3. have read   8. were cheering
4. is painting   9. will remember
5. are working   10. has inspired

B. 1. am reading   4. will fight
2. is practicing   5. am rooting
3. are traveling

Page 39

1. weighed   had   6. surprise   will   11. forgetting   was
2. expected   have   7. urging   are   12. cheering   were
3. becoming   is   8. flying   is   13. captured   had
4. stopped   has   9. lunged   has   14. changed   has
5. noticing   are   10. thinking   is   15. tell   will

Page 40

1. c   3. a   5. a   7. c   9. b
2. b   4. c   6. a   8. c   10. a

Page 41

A. 1. thought   6. paid   11. found
2. found   7. caught   12. paid
3. brought   8. held   13. caught
4. met   9. thought   14. kept
5. said   10. kept   15. met

B. Answers will vary.

Page 42

1. come   5. took   9. stolen   13. sprang
2. spoke   6. written   10. found   14. said
3. found   7. chosen   11. caught   15. built
4. sang   8. frozen   12. lost

Page 43

1. c   3. a   5. b   7. c   9. b
2. c   4. b   6. c   8. a   10. b

Page 44

A. 1. (Savannah and Elana), They   4. (barn), it
2. I, (David)   5. (Frank), he
3. (Melanie), She

B. 2. They, it   They = Many people, it = book
3. We, I   We = Amy and Duncan, I = Amy
4. She, them   She = Emma, them = eggs

Page 45

1. They
2. It
3. He
4. him
5. She
6. her
7. it
8. We
9. us
10. them
11. her
12. she
13. them
14. it

Page 46

A. 1. b   2. c   3. c   4. a   5. b
B. 1. a   2. a   3. c   4. b   5. b

Page 47

A.
1. (neighbor) him
2. (roses) They
3. (garden) It
4. (holes) them
5. (woodcutter) you
6. (woodcutter) he

B.
1. him : O
2. I : S, you : O, she : S
3. We : S, us : O
4. They : S, them : O
5. he : S, it : O
6. I : S, her : O
7. I : S, me : O

Page 48

1. him
2. her
3. she
4. They
5. them
6. I
7. We
8. He
9. her
10. They
11. me
12. him
13. me
14. them
15. He

Page 49

A. 1. a   2. c   3. b   4. c   5. a
B. 1. c   2. a   3. b   4. b   5. a

Page 50

A.
1. (My) family
2. (our) attic
3. (their) honeymoon
4. (her) first bicycle
5. (his) diary
6. (its) key
7. (your) house

B.
1. my
2. your
3. his
4. her
5. its
6. our
7. their

C. Answers will vary.

Page 51

A. 1. their   2. her   3. my   4. mine   5. her
B.
1. Which dresses in the closet are hers?
2. This is their collection of dried flowers.
3. I am enjoying his book.
4. Her disappointment showed clearly.
5. Is this his idea of a joke?

Page 52

A. 1. b   2. a   3. b   4. c   5. a
B. 1. b   2. b   3. b   4. b   5. c

Page 53

A.
1. conductor beats — S
2. musicians memorize — P
3. violinist leads — S
4. concert hall buzzes — S
5. Mariachi bands consist — P
6. singers and lead guitarist practice — P
7. Jazz groups perform — P
8. pianist works — S

B.
1. play
2. goes
3. takes
4. writes
5. watches
6. has
7. listen
8. visit

Page 54

A. 1. persuade   2. studies   3. describe   4. arrives   5. watches   6. replies   7. paints   8. flies   9. end   10. attend
B. Answers will vary.   C. Answers will vary.

Page 55

A.
1. "Can't we stay up just five more minutes?"
2. "That's another story."
3. "What's for lunch?"
4. "I am so excited!"

B.
1. Poissant said, "I remember once when Duke Ellington stayed at my house."
2. "Was Duke Ellington famous?" Punkin asked.
3. "He sure was!" Miss Ida exclaimed.
4. "I not only met him," Poissant explained, "but I was sitting in the parlor when he sat down at the piano and started to play."

C.
1. "Duke's playing sure heated up that little room!" exclaimed Poissant.
2. "Did any other famous people stay at your house?" asked Freda.
3. "No," said Poissant, "but Lena Horne once stayed at Miss Jackson's house."
4. Then he added, "However, that is a story for another day."

Page 56

A. 1. a. direct   2. a. indirect
    b. indirect   b. direct

B.
1. Franklin Delano Roosevelt stated, "the only thing we have to fear is fear itself."
2. "You must do the thing you think you cannot do," Eleanor Roosevelt advised.
3. "whoever is happy will make others happy," Anne Frank wrote.
4. "If winter comes, can spring be far behind?" asked the poet Shelley.
5. Mark Twain joked, "everyone talks about the weather, but no one does anything about it."

C.
1. "I'm glad you came," I said.
2. John asked me, "What did you think of the movie?"

Page 57

A. Sample answers are given.
1. thrilling
2. crooked
3. exciting
4. adorable
5. an, view
6. a, painting
7. an, movie
8. a, shirt

B.
1. Alice visited an interesting (museum).
2. The (museum) was filled with fascinating (art).
3. The (guide) provided detailed (descriptions).
4. The bronze (statue) was her (favorite).
5. One entire (floor) was devoted to bright (paintings) of blue (flowers).
6. The top (floor) contained ten enormous (sculptures).
7. The (museum) is a popular tourist (stop).
8. Visitors can buy a delicious (lunch) in the (cafeteria).
9. Beautiful (gifts) are sold in the (shop).
10. Many (visitors) spend a full (day) in the (museum).

Page 58

A.
1. in Nebraska, where
2. during the summer, when
3. to the neighborhood pool, where
4. in the afternoon, when
5. in the ocean, where

B.
1. Gerard is giving a party (for Maria).
2. Norma sent invitations (to all their friends).
3. The food was made (by Josue).
4. Rebecca decorated the room (with streamers).
5. Mela sat next (to Danielle).
6. Kama played a song (on her guitar).
7. Terry arrived late (with Deborah).
8. Adriane brought a huge chocolate cake (from the bakery).
9. The celebration lasted (until dinnertime).
10. Sarah and Joanna took the train home (with Liza).

Page 59

A.
more slowly, most slowly
more gracefully, most gracefully
more fiercely, most fiercely
more swiftly, most swiftly
Sample answers are given.
1. the most gracefully of all mammals.
2. more slowly than a snake.
3. the most fiercely of all the dinosaurs.

B.
1. Anna (jumped) quickly into the pool.
2. Danny (sat) quietly on the sidelines.
3. The dog gently (pushed) open the door.
4. The animal (waited) patiently to be fed.
5. Laurie tenderly (petted) the puppy.
6. The crowd (cheered) loudly when the team scored a goal.
7. Joseph (told) him later about the party.
8. Lucy immediately (volunteered) to make invitations.
9. The cat boldly (climbed) the tree.

Page 60

A. Answers will vary.
B.
1. Luke, Sam, and Nick are putting on a play.
2. The play will begin at 8:00 PM.
3. Yalixa, his sister, wrote the play.
4. correct
5. Amy, can you make the costumes?
6. Like her mom, Luisa is a good singer.
7. Our flag is red, white, and blue.
8. correct
9. Nathan will visit on March 28, 2004.
10. We are always happy when he comes, but sad when he leaves.

Page 61

A.

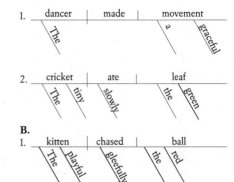

1.
The	dancer	made	movement

(a graceful)

2.
The	cricket	ate	leaf

(tiny, slowly, the green)

B.
1.
The	kitten	chased	ball

(playful, gleefully, the red)